Stewart Kidd Dramatic Anthologies

Fifty Contemporary One-Act Plays

Edited by
FRANK SHAY and PIERRE LOVING

THIS volume contains FIFTY REPRESENTATIVE ONE-ACT PLAYS of the MODERN THEATER, chosen from the dramatic works of contemporary writers all over the world and is the second volume in the *Stewart Kidd Dramatic Anthologies*, the first being European Theories of the Drama, by Barrett H Clark, which has been so enthusiastically received.

The editors have scrupulously sifted countless plays and have selected the best available in English. One-half the plays have never before been published in book form; thirty-one are no longer available in any other edition.

The work satisfies a long-felt want for a handy collection of the choicest plays produced by the art theaters all over the world. It is a complete repertory for a little theater, a volume for the study of the modern drama, a representative collection of the world's best short plays.

CONTENTS

AUSTRIA
Schnitzler (Arthur)—Literature
BELGIUM
Maeterlinck (Maurice)—The Intruder
BOLIVIA
More (Federico)—Interlude
FRANCE
Ancey (George)—M. Lamblin
Porto-Riche (Georges) — Francoise's Luck
GERMANY
Ettinger (Karl)—Altruism
von Hofmannsthal (Hugo)—Madonna Dianora
Wedekind (Frank)—The Tenor
GREAT BRITAIN
Bennett (Arnold)—A Good Woman
Calderon (George)—The Little Stone House.
Cannan (Gilbert)—Mary's Wedding
Dowson (Ernest)—The Pierrot of the Minute.
Ellis (Mrs. Havelock)—The Subjection of Kezia
Hankin (St. John)—The Constant Lover
INDIA
Mukerji (Dhan Gopal)—The Judgment of Indra
IRELAND
Gregory (Lady)—The Workhouse Ward
HOLLAND
Speenhoff (J. H.)—Louise
HUNGARY
Biro (Lajos)—The Grandmother
ITALY
Giocosa (Giuseppe)—The Rights of the Soul
RUSSIA
Andreyev (Leonid)—Love of One's Neighbor
Tchekoff (Anton)—The Boor

SPAIN
Benevente (Jacinto)—His Widow's Husband
Quinteros (Serafina and Joaquin Alverez)—A Sunny Morning
SWEDEN
Strindberg (August)—The Creditor
Wied (Gustave)—Autumn Fires
UNITED STATES
Beach (Lewis)—Brothers
Cowan (Sada)—In the Morgue
Crocker (Bosworth)—The Baby Carriage
Cronyn (George W.)—A Death in Fever Flat
Davies (Mary Carolyn)—The Slave with Two Faces
Day (Frederick L.)—The Slump
Flanner (Hildegard)—Mansions
Glaspell (Susan)—Trifles
Gerstenberg (Alice)—The Pot Boiler
Helburn (Theresa)—Enter the Hero
Hudson (Holland)—The Shepherd in the Distance
Kemp (Harry)—Boccaccio's Untold Tale
Langner (Lawrence)—Another Way Out
MacMillan (Mary)—The Shadowed Star
Millay (Edna St. Vincent)—Aro da Capo
Moeller (Philip)—Helena's Husband
O'Neill (Eugene)—Ile
Stevens (Thomas Wood)—The Nursery Maid of Heaven
Stevens (Wallace)—Three Travelers Watch a Sunrise
Tompkins (Frank G.)—Sham
Walker (Stuart)—The Medicine Show
Wellman (Rita)—For All Time
Wilde (Percival)—The Finger of God
YIDDISH
Ash (Sholom)—Night
Pinski (David)—Forgotten Souls

Large 8vo, 585 pages   Net, $5.00

Send for Complete Dramatic Catalogue

STEWART KIDD COMPANY
PUBLISHERS,   -   -   CINCINNATI, U. S. A.

STEWART KIDD MODERN PLAYS
Edited by Frank Shay

Cornell University Library
PS 3507.E44S9
Sweet and twenty, a comedy in one act, by

3 1924 022 352 870

SWEET AND TWENTY

Stewart Kidd Modern Plays

Edited by FRANK SHAY

To meet the immensely increased demands of the play-reading public and those interested in the modern drama, Stewart Kidd are issuing under the general editorship of Frank Shay a series of plays from the pens of the world's best contemporary writers No effort is being spared to secure the best work available, and the plays are issued in a form that is at once attractive to readers and suited to the needs of the performer and producer *Buffalo Express*. "Each play is of merit Each is unlike the other The group furnishes a striking example [of the realistic trend of the modern drama "

From time to time special announcements will be printed giving complete lists of the plays

SHAM, a Social Satire in One Act *By Frank G Tompkins*
Originally produced by Sam Hume, at the Arts and Crafts Theatre, Detroit

San Francisco Bulletin · "The lines are new and many of them are decidedly clever"

Providence Journal · "An ingenious and merry little one-act play'

THE SHEPHERD IN THE DISTANCE, a Pantomime in One Act. *By Holland Hudson.*
Originally produced by the Washington Square Players.

Oakland Tribune. "A pleasing pantomime of the Ancient East '

MANSIONS, a Play in One Act. *By Hildegarde Flanner.*
Originally produced by the Indiana Little Theatre Society.

Three Arts Magazine. "This thoughtful and well-written play of Characters and Ideals has become a favorite with Little Theatres and is now available in print"

HEARTS TO MEND, a Fantasy in One Act.
By H A. Overstreet.

Originally produced by the Fireside Players, White Plains, N Y

St Louis Star · "It is a light whimsy and well carried out."

San Francisco Chronicle. "No one is likely to hear or read it without real and legitimate pleasure"

SIX WHO PASS WHILE THE LENTILS BOIL.
By Stuart Walker.

Originally produced by the Portmanteau Players at Christodora House, New York City

Brooklyn Eagle "Literary without being pedantic, and dramatic

Sweet and Twenty

A Comedy in One Act

By
FLOYD DELL
Author of
MOON CALF

First produced by the Provincetown Players, New York City January 25, 1918, with the following cast:

THE YOUNG WOMAN	*Edna St Vincent Millay*
THE YOUNG MAN -	*Ordway Tead*
THE AGENT - -	*Otto Liveright*
THE GUARD - -	*- Louis Ell*

CINCINNATI
STEWART KIDD COMPANY
PUBLISHERS

COPYRIGHT, 1921
STEWART & KIDD COMPANY

All rights reserved
COPYRIGHT IN ENGLAND

SWEET AND TWENTY is fully protected by the copyright law, all requirements of which have been complied with. No performance, either professional or amateur, may be given without the written permission of the author or his representative, Stewart Kidd Company, Cincinnati, Ohio.

Sweet and Twenty

Scene—*A corner of the cherry orchard on the country place of the late Mr. Boggley, now on sale and open for inspection to prospective buyers. The cherry orchard, now in full bloom, is a very pleasant place. There is a green-painted rustic bench beside the path. . . .*

(*This scene can be effectively produced on a small stage by a back-drop painted a blue-green color, with a single conventionalized cherry branch painted across it, and two three-leaved screens masking the wings, painted in blue-green with a spray of cherry blossoms*).

A young woman, dressed in a light summer frock and carrying a parasol, drifts in from the back. She sees the bench, comes over to it and sits down with an air of petulant weariness.

A handsome young man enters from the right. He stops short in surprise on seeing the charming stranger who lolls upon the bench. He takes off his hat.

HE

Oh, I beg your pardon!

SHE

Oh, you needn't! I've no right to be here, either.

HE

(*Coming down to her*) Now what do you mean by that?

SHE

I thought perhaps you were playing truant, as I am.

SWEET AND TWENTY

HE
   Playing truant?
SHE
   I was looking at the house, you know. And I got tired and ran away.
HE
   Well, to tell the truth, so did I. It's dull work, isn't it?
SHE
   I've been upstairs and down for two hours. That family portrait gallery finished me. It was so old and gloomy and dead that I felt as if I were dead myself. I just had to do something. I wanted to jab my parasol through the window-pane. I understood just how the suffragettes felt. But I was afraid of shocking the agent. He is such a meek little man, and he seemed to think so well of me. If I had broken the window I would have shattered his ideals of womanhood, too, I'm afraid. So I just slipped away quietly and came here.
HE
   I've only been there half an hour and we—I've only been in the basement. That's why our tours of inspection didn't bring us together sooner. I've been cross-examining the furnace. Do you understand furnaces? (*He sits down beside her*) I don't.
SHE
   Do you like family portraits? I hate 'em!
HE
   What! Do the family portraits go with the house?

SWEET AND TWENTY

SHE

No, thank heaven. They've been bequeathed to the Metropolitan Museum of Horrors, I understand. They're valuable historically—early colonial governors and all that sort of stuff. But there is someone with me who—who takes a deep interest in such things.

HE

(*frowning at a sudden memory*) Hm. Didn't I see you at that real estate office in New York yesterday?

SHE

Yes. *He* was with me then.

HE (*compassionately*)

I—I thought I remembered seeing you with—with him

SHE (*cheerfully*)

Isn't he *just* the sort of man who would be interested in family portraits?

HE (*confused*)

Well—since you ask me—I—!

SHE

Oh, that's all right. Tubby's a dear, in spite of his funny old ideas. I like him very much.

HE

(*gulping the pill*) Yes. . . .

SHE

He's so anxious to please me in buying this house. I suppose it's all right to have a house, but I'd like to become acquainted with it gradually. I'd like to feel that there was always some corner left to explore—some mystery

SWEET AND TWENTY

saved up for a rainy day. Tubby can't understand that. He drags me everywhere, explaining how we'll keep this and change that—dormer windows here and perhaps a new wing there. . . . I suppose you've been rebuilding the house, too?

HE

No. Merely decided to turn that sunny south room into a study. It would make a very pleasant place to work. But if you really want the place, I'd hate to take it away from you.

SHE

I was just going to say that if *you* really wanted it, *I'd* withdraw. It was Tubby's idea to buy it, you know—not mine. You *do* want it, don't you?

HE

I can't say that I do. It's so infernally big. But Maria thinks I ought to have it. (*Explanatorily*) Maria is—

SHE (*gently*)

She's—the one who *is* interested in furnaces, I understand. I saw her with you at the real-estate office yesterday. Well—furnaces are necessary, I suppose. (*There is a pause, which she breaks suddenly*) Do you see that bee?

HE

A bee? (*He follows her gaze up to a cluster of blossoms.*)

SHE

Yes—there! (*Affectionately*) The rascal! There he goes. (*Their eyes follow the flight of the bee across the orchard. There is a silence, in which*

SWEET AND TWENTY

Maria and Tubby drift into the limbo of forgotten things. Alone together beneath the blossoms, a spell seems to have fallen upon them. She tries to think of something to say—and at last succeeds.)

SHE

Have you heard the story of the people who used to live here?

HE

No; why?

SHE

An agent was telling us. It's quite romantic—and rather sad. You see, the man that built this house was in love with a girl. He was building it for her—as a surprise. But he had neglected to mention to her that he was in love with her. And so, in pique, she married another man, though she was really in love with him. The news came just when he had finished the house. He shut it up for a year or two, but eventually married someone else, and they lived here for ten years—most unhappily. Then they went abroad, and the house was sold. It was bought, curiously enough, by the husband of the girl he had been in love with. They lived here till they died—hating each other to the end, the agent says.

HE

It gives me the shivers. To think of that house, haunted by the memories of wasted love! Which of us, I wonder, will have to live in it? I don't want to.

SHE *(prosaically)*

Oh, don't take it so seriously as all that. If

SWEET AND TWENTY

one can't live in a house where there's been an unhappy marriage, why, good heavens, where *is* one going to live? Most marriages, I fancy, are unhappy.

HE

A bitter philosophy for one so—

SHE

Nonsense! But listen to the rest of the story. The most interesting part is about this very orchard.

HE

Really!

SHE

Yes. This orchard, it seems, was here before the house was. It was part of an old farm where he and she—the unhappy lovers, you know—stopped one day, while they were out driving, and asked for something to eat. The farmer's wife was busy, but she gave them each a glass of milk, and told them they could eat all the cherries they wanted. So they picked a hatful of cherries, and ate them, sitting on a bench like this one. And then he fell in love with her. . . .

HE

And . . . didn't tell her so. . . . (*She glances at him in alarm. His self-possession has vanished. He is pale and frightened, but there is a desperate look in his eyes, as if some unknown power were forcing him to do something very rash. In short, he seems like a young man who has just fallen in love.*)

SWEET AND TWENTY

SHE (*hastily*)
  So you see this orchard is haunted, too!
HE
  I feel it. I seem to hear the ghost of that old-time lover whispering to me. . . .
SHE (*provocatively*)
  Indeed! What does he say?
HE
  He says: "I was a coward; you must be bold. I was silent; you must speak out."
SHE (*mischievously*)
  That's very curious—because that old lover isn't dead at all. He's a baronet or something in England.
HE (*earnestly*)
  His youth is dead; and it is his youth that speaks to me.
SHE (*quickly*)
  You mustn't believe all that ghosts tell you.
HE
  Oh, but I must. For they know the folly of silence—the bitterness of cowardice.
SHE
  The circumstances were—slightly—different, weren't they?
HE (*stubbornly*)
  I don't care!
SHE (*soberly*)
  You know perfectly well it's no use.
HE
  I can't help that!

SWEET AND TWENTY

SHE
Please! You simply mustn't! It's disgraceful!
HE
What's disgraceful?
SHE (*confused*)
What you are going to say.
HE (*simply*)
Only that I love you. What is there disgraceful about that? It's beautiful!
SHE
It's wrong.
HE
It's inevitable.
SHE
Why inevitable? Can't you talk with a girl in a cherry orchard for half an hour without falling in love with her?
HE
Not if the girl is you.
SHE
But why especially *me?*
HE
I don't know. Love—is a mystery. I only know that I was destined to love you.
SHE
How can you be so sure?
HE
Because you have changed the world for me. It's as though I had been groping about in the dark, and then—sunrise! And there's a queer feeling here. (*He puts his hand on his heart*) To tell the honest truth, there's a still queerer

feeling in the pit of my stomach. It's a gone feeling, if you must know. And my knees are weak. I know now why men used to fall on their knees when they told a girl they loved her; it was because they couldn't stand up. And there's a feeling in my feet as though I were walking on air. And—

SHE (*faintly*)
That's enough!

HE
And I could die for you and be glad of the chance. It's perfectly absurd, but it's absolutely true. I've never spoken to you before, and heaven knows I may never get a chance to speak to you again, but I'd never forgive myself if I didn't say this to you now. I love you! love you! love you! Now tell me I'm a fool. Tell me to go. Anything—I've said my say. . . . Why don't you speak?

SHE
I—I've nothing to say—except—except that I—well— (*almost inaudibly*) I feel some of those symptoms myself.

HE (*triumphantly*)
You love me!

SHE
I—don't know. Yes. Perhaps.

HE
Then kiss me!

SHE (*doubtfully*)
No. . . .

HE
Kiss me!

SWEET AND TWENTY

SHE (*tormentedly*)
  Oh, what's the use?
HE
  I don't know. I don't care. I only know that we love each other.
SHE
  (*after a moment's hesitation, desperately*) I don't care, either! I *do* want to kiss you. (*She does. . . . He is the first to awake from the ecstasy.*)
HE
  It is wicked—
SHE (*absently*)
  Is it?
HE
  But, oh heaven! kiss me again! (*She does.*)
SHE
  Darling!
HE
  Do you suppose anyone is likely to come this way?
SHE
  No.
HE (*speculatively*) Your husband is probably still in the portrait gallery. . . .
SHE
  My husband! (*Drawing away*) What do you mean? (*Thoroughly awake now*) You didn't think—? (*She jumps up and laughs convulsively*) He thought poor old Tubby was my husband!!
HE
  (*staring up at her bewildered*) Why, isn't he your husband?

SWEET AND TWENTY

SHE (*scornfully*)
  No!! He's my uncle!

HE
  Your unc—

SHE
  Yes, of course! (*Indignantly*) Do you suppose I would be married to a man that's fat and bald and forty years old?

HE (*distressed*)
  I—I beg your pardon. I did think so.

SHE
  Just because you saw me with him? How ridiculous!

HE
  It was a silly mistake. But—the things you said! You spoke so—realistically—about marriage.

SHE
  It was *your* marriage I was speaking about. (*With hasty compunction*) Oh, I beg your—

HE
  My marriage! (*He rises*) Good heavens! And to whom, pray, did you think I was married? (*A light dawning*) To Maria? Why, Maria is my aunt!

SHE
  Yes—of course. How stupid of me.

HE
  Let's get this straight. Are you married to *anybody?*

SHE
  Certainly not. As if I would let anybody make love to me if I were!

SWEET AND TWENTY

HE
>Now don't put on airs. You did something quite as improper. You kissed a married man.

SHE
>I didn't.

HE
>It's the same thing. You *thought* I was married.

SHE
>But you *aren't*.

HE
>No. I'm *not* married. And—and—*you're* not married. (*The logic of the situation striking him all of a sudden*) In fact—! (*He pauses, rather alarmed.*)

SHE
>Yes?

HE
>In fact—well—there's no reason in the world why we *shouldn't* make love to each other!

SHE
>(*equally startled*) Why—that's so!

HE
>Then—then—shall we?

SHE
>(*sitting down and looking demurely at her toes*) Oh, not if you don't want to!

HE
>(*adjusting himself to the situation*) Well—under the circumstances—I suppose I ought to begin by asking you to marry me. . . .

SHE
>(*languidly, with a provoking glance*) You don't seem very anxious to.

SWEET AND TWENTY

HE
  (*feeling at a disadvantage*) It isn't that—but—well—
SHE (*lightly*)
  Well what?
HE
  Dash it all, I don't know your name!
SHE
  (*looking at him with wild curiosity*) That didn't seem to stop you a while ago. . . .
HE (*doggedly*)
  Well, then—will you marry me?
SHE (*promptly*)
  No.
HE (*surprised*)
  No! Why do you say that?
SHE (*coolly*)
  Why should I marry you? I know nothing about you. I've known you for less than an hour.
HE (*sardonically*)
  That fact didn't seem to keep you from kissing me.
SHE
  Besides—I don't like the way you go about it. If you'd propose the same way you made love to me, maybe I'd accept you.
HE
  All right. (*Dropping on one knee before her*) Beloved! (*An awkward pause*) No, I can't do it. (*He gets up and distractedly dusts off his knees with his handkerchief*) I'm very sorry.

SWEET AND TWENTY

SHE

(*with calm inquiry*) Perhaps it's because you don't love me any more?

HE (*fretfully*)

Of course I love you!

SHE (*coldly*)

But you don't want to marry me. . . . I see.

HE

Not at all! I *do* want to marry you. But—

SHE

Well?

HE

Marriage is a serious matter. Now don't take offense! I only meant that—well— (*He starts again*) We *are* in love with each other, and that's the important thing. But, as you said, we don't know each other. I've no doubt that when we get acquainted we will like each other better still. But we've got to get acquainted first.

SHE (*rising*)

You're just like Tubby buying a house. You want to know all about it. Well! I warn you that you'll never know all about me. So you needn't try.

HE (*apologetically*)

It was *your* suggestion.

SHE (*impatiently*)

Oh, all right! Go ahead and cross-examine me if you like. I'll tell you to begin with that I'm perfectly healthy, and that there's no T. B.,

SWEET AND TWENTY

insanity, or Socialism in my family. What else do you want to know?

HE (*hesitantly*)
Why did you put Socialism in?

SHE
Oh, just for fun. You aren't a Socialist, are you?

HE
Yes. (*Earnestly*) Do you know what Socialism is?

SHE (*innocently*)
It's the same thing as Anarchy, isn't it?

HE (*gently*)
No. At least not my kind. I believe in municipal ownership of street cars, and all that sort of thing. I'll give you some books to read

SHE
Well, I never ride in street cars, so I don't care whether they're municipally owned or not. By the way, do you dance?

HE
No.

SHE
You must learn right away. I can't bother to teach you myself, but I know where you can get private lessons and become really good in a month. It is stupid not to be able to dance.

HE
(*as if he had tasted quinine*) I can see myself doing the tango! Grr!

SHE
The tango went out long ago, my dear.

SWEET AND TWENTY

HE
>(*with great decision*) Well—I *won't* learn to dance. You might as well know that to begin with.

SHE
>And I won't read your old books on Socialism. You might as well know *that to begin with!*

HE
>Come, come! This will never do. You see, my dear, it's simply that I *can't* dance, and there's no use for me to try to learn.

SHE
>Anybody can learn. I've made expert dancers out of the awkwardest men!

HE
>But, you see, I've no inclination toward dancing. It's out of my world.

SHE
>And I've no inclination toward municipal ownership. *It's* out of *my* world!

HE
>It ought not to be out of the world of any intelligent person.

SHE
>(*turning her back on him*) All right—if you want to call me stupid!

HE
>(*turning and looking away meditatively*) It appears that we have very few tastes in common.

SHE
>(*tapping her foot*) So it seems.

HE
>If we married we might be happy for a month—

SWEET AND TWENTY

SHE
  Perhaps. (*They remain standing with their backs to each other.*)
HE
  And then—the old story. Quarrels. . . .
SHE
  I never could bear quarrels. . . .
HE
  An unhappy marriage. . . .
SHE
  (*realizing it*) Oh!
HE
  (*hopelessly turning toward her*) I can't marry you.
SHE
  (*recovering quickly and facing him with a smile*) Nobody asked you, sir, she said!
HE
  (*with a gesture of finality*) Well—there seems to be no more to say.
SHE (*sweetly*)
  Except good-bye.
HE (*firmly*)
  Good-bye, then. (*He holds out his hand.*)
SHE
  (*taking it*) Good-bye!
HE
  (*taking her other hand—after a pause, helplessly*) Good-bye!
SHE
  (*drawing in his eyes*) Good-bye! (*They cling to each other, and are presently lost in a passionate embrace. He breaks loose and stamps away, then turns to her.*)

SWEET AND TWENTY

HE
  Damn it all, we *do* love each other!
SHE
  (*wiping her eyes*) What a pity that is the only taste we have in common!
HE
  Do you suppose that is enough?
SHE
  I wish it were!
HE
  A month of happiness—
SHE
  Yes!
HE
  And then—wretchedness.
SHE
  No—never!
HE
  We mustn't do it.
SHE
  I suppose not.
HE
  Come, let us control ourselves.
SHE
  Yes, let's. (*They take hands again.*)
HE
  (*with an effort*) I wish you happiness. I—I'll go to Europe for a year. Try to forget me.
SHE
  I shall be married when you get back—perhaps.
HE
  I hope it's somebody that's not bald and fat and forty. Otherwise—!

SWEET AND TWENTY

SHE
And you—for goodness sake! marry a girl that's very young and very, very pretty. That will help.

HE
We mustn't prolong this. If we stay together another minute—

SHE
Then go!

HE
I can't go!

SHE
You must, darling! You must!

HE
Oh, if somebody would only come along! (*They are leaning toward each other, dizzy upon the brink of another kiss, when somebody does come—a short, mild-looking man in a Derby hat. There is an odd gleam in his eyes*).

THE INTRUDER (*startled*)
Excuse me! (*They turn and stare at him, but their hands cling fast to each other.*)

SHE (*faintly*)
The Agent!

THE AGENT
(*in despairing accents*) Too late! Too late!

THE YOUNG MAN
No! Just in time!

THE AGENT
Too late, I say! I will go. (*He turns.*)

THE YOUNG MAN
No! Stay!

SWEET AND TWENTY

THE AGENT
　What's the use? It has already begun. What good can I do now?

THE YOUNG MAN
　I'll show you what good you can do now. Come here! (*The Agent approaches*) Can you unloose my hands from those of this young woman?

THE YOUNG WOMAN
　(*haughtily releasing herself and walking away*) You needn't trouble! I can do it myself.

THE YOUNG MAN
　Thank you. It was utterly beyond my power. (*To the Agent*) Will you kindly take hold of me and move me over *there*? (*The Agent propels him away from the girl*) Thank you. At this distance I can perhaps make my farewell in a seemly and innocuous manner.

THE AGENT
　Young man, you will not say farewell to that young lady for ten days—and perhaps never!

THE YOUNG WOMAN
　What!

THE AGENT
　They have arranged it all.

THE YOUNG MAN
　Who has arranged *what*?

THE AGENT
　Your aunt, Miss Brooke—and (*to the young woman*) your uncle, Mr. Egerton— (*The young people turn and stare at each other in amazement.*)

THE YOUNG MAN
　Egerton! Are you Helen Egerton?

SWEET AND TWENTY

HELEN
   And are you George Brooke?
THE AGENT
   Your aunt and uncle have just discovered each other up at the house, and they have arranged for you all to take dinner together to-night, and then go to a ten-day house-party at Mr. Egerton's place on Long Island. (*Grimly*) The reason of all this will be plain to you. They want you two to get married.
GEORGE
   Then we're done for! We'll have to get married now whether we want to or not!
HELEN
   What! Just to please *them?* I shan't do it!
GEORGE (*gloomily*)
   You don't know my Aunt Maria.
HELEN
   And Tubby will try to bully me, I suppose. But I won't do it—no matter what he says!
THE AGENT
   Pardon what may seem an impertinence, Miss; but is it really true that you don't want to marry this young man?
HELEN (*flaming*)
   I suppose because you saw me in his arms—! Oh, I want to, all right, but—
THE AGENT (*mildly*)
   Then what seems to be the trouble?
HELEN
   I—oh, you explain to him, George. (*She goes to the bench and sits down.*)

SWEET AND TWENTY

GEORGE

Well, it's this way. As you may have deduced from what you saw, we are madly in love with each other—

HELEN

(*from the bench*) But I'm not madly in love with municipal ownership. That's the chief difficulty.

GEORGE

No, the chief difficulty is that I refuse to entertain even a platonic affection for the tango.

HELEN (*irritably*)

I told you the tango had gone out long ago!

GEORGE

Well, then, the maxixe.

HELEN

Stupid!

GEORGE

And there you have it! No doubt it seems ridiculous to you.

THE AGENT (*gravely*)

Not at all, my boy. I've known marriage to go to smash on far less than that. When you come to think of it, a taste for dancing and a taste for municipal ownership stand at the two ends of the earth away from each other. They represent two different ways of taking life. And if two people who live in the same house can't agree on those two things, they'd disagree on ten thousand things that came up every day. And what's the use for two different kinds of beings to try to live together? It doesn't work,

SWEET AND TWENTY

no matter how much love there is between them.

GEORGE

(*rushing up to him in surprise and gratification, and shaking his hand warmly*) Then you're our friend. You will help us not to get married!

THE AGENT

Your aunt is very set on it—and your uncle, too, Miss!

HELEN

We must find some way to get out of it, or they'll have us cooped up together in that house before we know it. (*Rising and coming over to the Agent*) Can't you think up some scheme?

THE AGENT

Perhaps I can, and perhaps I can't. I'm a bachelor myself, Miss, and that means that I've thought up many a scheme to get out of marriage myself.

HELEN (*outraged*)

You old scoundrel!

THE AGENT

Oh, it's not so bad as you may think, Miss. I've always gone through the marriage ceremony to please them. But that's not what I call marriage.

GEORGE

Then what do you call marriage?

HELEN

Yes, I'd like to know!

SWEET AND TWENTY

THE AGENT

Marriage, my young friends, is an iniquitous arrangement devised by the Devil himself for driving all the love out of the hearts of lovers. They start out as much in love with each other as you two are to-day, and they end by being as sick of the sight of each other as you two will be twenty years hence if I don't find a way of saving you alive out of the Devil's own trap. It's not lack of love that's the trouble with marriage—it's marriage itself. And when I say marriage, I don't mean promising to love, honor, and obey, for richer, for poorer, in sickness and in health till death do you part—that's only human nature to wish and to attempt. And it might be done if it weren't for the iniquitous arrangement of marriage.

GEORGE (*puzzled*)

But what *is* the iniquitous arrangement?

THE AGENT

Ah, that's the trouble! If I tell you, you won't believe me. You'll go ahead and try it out, and find out what all the unhappy ones have found out before you. Listen to me, my children. Did you ever go on a picnic? (*He looks from one to the other—they stand astonished and silent*) Of course you have. Everyone has. There is an instinct in us which makes us go back to the ways of our savage ancestors—to gather about a fire in the forest, to cook meat on a pointed stick, and eat it with our fingers. But how many books would you write, young man, if you had to go back to the camp-fire every day for your lunch? And how many new dances would *you* invent if you lived eternally in the picnic stage of civilization? No! the picnic is incompatible with everyday living. As incompatible as marriage.

GEORGE
But—

HELEN
But—

THE AGENT
Marriage is the nest-building instinct, turned by the Devil himself into an institution to hold the human soul in chains. The whole story of marriage is told in the old riddle: "Why do birds in their nests agree? Because if they don't, they'll fall out." That's it. Marriage is a nest so small that there is no room in it for disagreement. Now it may be all right for birds to agree, but human beings are not built that way. They disagree, and home becomes a little hell. Or else they do agree, at the expense of the soul's freedom stifled in one or both.

HELEN
Yes, but tell me—

GEORGE
Ssh!

THE AGENT
Yet there *is* the nest-building instinct. You feel it, both of you. If you don't now, you will as soon as you are married. If you are fools, you will try to live all your lives in a love-nest; and you will imprison your souls within it, and the Devil will laugh.

SWEET AND TWENTY

HELEN

(*to George*) I am beginning to be afraid of him.

GEORGE

So am I.

THE AGENT

If you are wise, you will build yourselves a little nest secretly in the woods, away from civilization, and you will run away together to that nest whenever you are in the mood. A nest so small that it will hold only two beings and one thought—the thought of love. And then you will come back refreshed to civilization, where every soul is different from every other soul—you will let each other alone, forget each other, and do your own work in peace. Do you understand?

HELEN

He means we should occupy separate sides of the house, I think. Or else that we should live apart and only see each other on week-ends. I'm not sure which.

THE AGENT (*passionately*)

I mean that you should not stifle love with civilization, nor encumber civilization with love. What have they to do with each other? You think you want a fellow student of economics. You are wrong. *You* think you want a dancing partner. You are mistaken. You want a revelation of the glory of the universe.

HELEN

(*to George, confidentially*) It's blithering nonsense, of course. But it *was* something like that—a while ago.

SWEET AND TWENTY

GEORGE (*bewilderedly*)
　Yes; when we knew it was our first kiss and thought it was to be our last.

THE AGENT (*fiercely*)
　A kiss is always the first kiss and the last—or it is nothing.

HELEN (*conclusively*)
　He's quite mad.

GEORGE
　Absolutely.

THE AGENT
　Mad? Of course I am mad. But— (*He turns suddenly, and subsides as a man in a guard's uniform enters.*)

THE GUARD
　Ah, here you are! Thought you'd given us the slip, did you? (*To the others*) Escaped from the Asylum, he did, a week ago, and got a job here. We've been huntin' him high and low. Come along now!

GEORGE
　(*recovering with difficulty the power of speech*)
What—what's the matter with him?

GUARD
　Matter with him? He went crazy, he did, readin' the works of Bernard Shaw. And if he wasn't in the insane asylum he'd be in jail. He's a bigamist, he is. He married fourteen women. But none of 'em would go on the witness stand against him. Said he was an ideal husband, they did. Fourteen of 'em! But otherwise he's perfectly harmless. Come now!

SWEET AND TWENTY

THE AGENT (*pleasantly*)
Perfectly harmless! Yes, perfectly harmless! (*He is led out.*)

HELEN
That explains it all!

GEORGE
Yes—and yet I feel there was something in what he was saying.

HELEN
Well—are we going to get married or not? We've got to decide that before we face my uncle and your aunt.

GEORGE
Of course we'll get married. You have your work and I mine, and—

HELEN
Well, if we do, then you can't have that sunny south room for a study. I want it for the nursery.

GEORGE
The nursery!

HELEN
Yes; babies, you know!

GEORGE
Good heavens!

[CURTAIN]

MORE SHORT PLAYS
By MARY MacMILLAN

Plays that act well may read well. Miss MacMillan's Plays are good reading. Nor is literary excellence a detriment to dramatic performance.

This volume contains eight Plays:

His Second Girl. One-act comedy, just before the Civil War. Interior, 45 minutes. Three women, three men.

At the Church Door. Fantastic farce, one act, 20 to 30 minutes. Interior. Present. Two women, two men.

Honey. Four short acts. Present, in the southern mountains. Same interior cabin scene throughout. Three women, one man, two girls.

The Dress Rehearsal of Hamlet. One-act costume farce. Present. Interior. Forty-five minutes. Ten women taking men's parts.

The Pioneers. Five very short acts. 1791 in Middle-West. Interior. Four men, five women, five children, five Indians.

In Mendelesia, Part I. Costume play, Middle Ages. Interior. Thirty minutes or more. Four women, one man-servant.

In Mendelesia, Part II. Modern realism of same plot. One act. Present. Interior. Thirty minutes. Four women, one maid-servant.

The Dryad. Fantasy in free verse, one act. Thirty minutes. Outdoors. Two women, one man. Present.

These plays, as well as SHORT PLAYS, have been presented by clubs and schools in Boston, New York, Buffalo, Detroit, Cleveland, New Orleans, San Francisco, etc., and by the Portmanteau Theatre, the Chicago Art Institute Theatre, the Denver Little Art Theatre, at Carmel-by-the-Sea in California, etc.

Handsomely bound and uniform with S. & K. Dramatic Series. 12mo. Cloth. Net, $2.50; ¾ Turkey Morocco, Net, $8.50.

STEWART & KIDD COMPANY
Publishers   Cincinnati, U. S. A.

CPSIA information can be obtained
at www.ICGtesting.com
Printed in the USA
LVHW081637251022
731536LV00004B/156